Sam Squit's Quarry in Court Cowlease, Harry Chinchen in background, Walter Brown in front - 1930

Purbeck Underground

David Pushman

"Inference has two aspects; it is both in the mind and in the facts".

(Logic: A.A. Luce)

To Jeannie

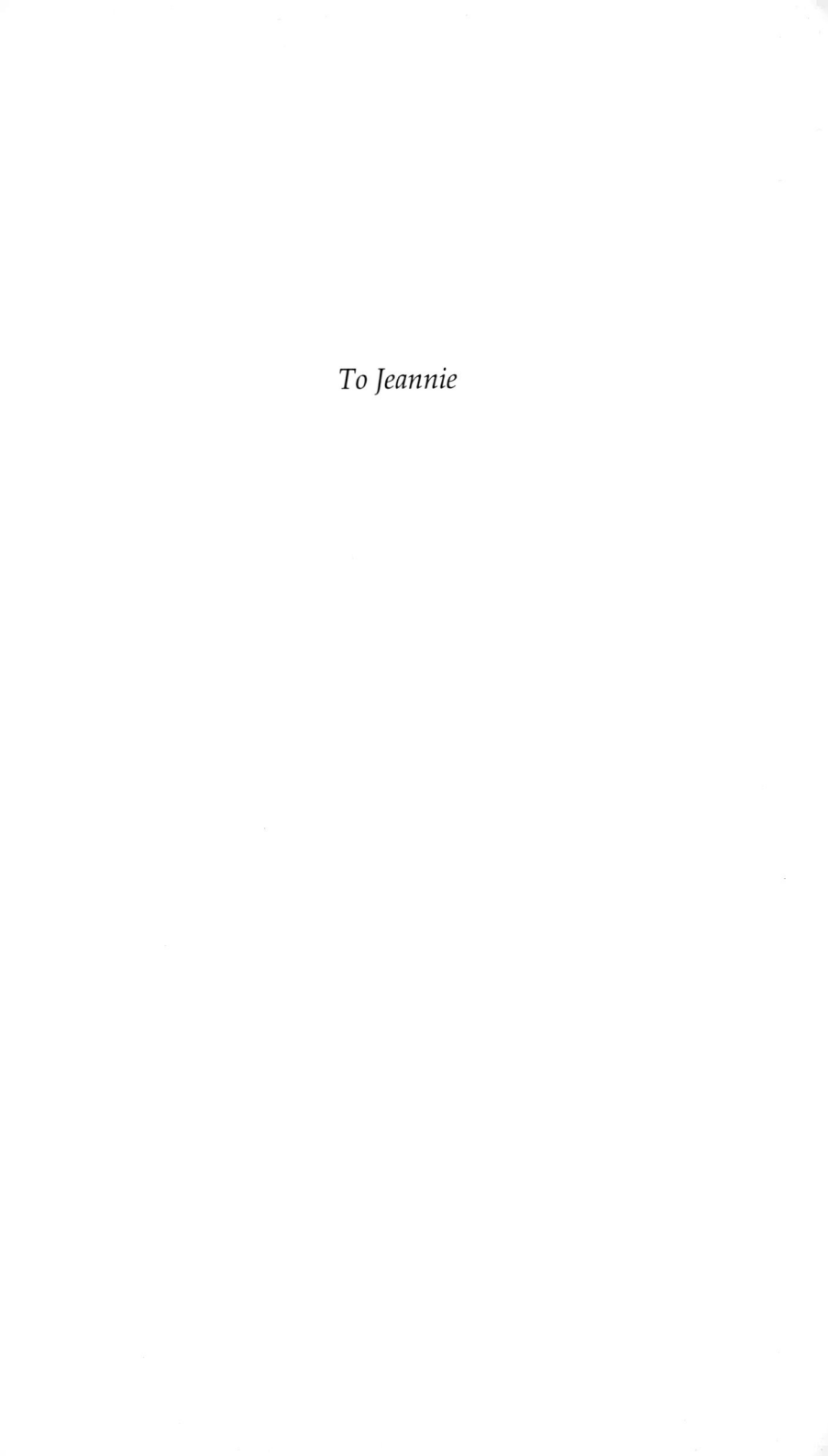

Other books by the same author

Precious Stone of Dorset
A Crown of Snow

PREFACE

So favourable has been the reception of my little book, that I am persuaded to publish a second edition.

I often listen to visitors as they walk along the streets, or as I sit in a corner of a pub, asking why? Why is Purbeck called an island when it is not? Why is Corfe Castle a ruin? Why don't they export Purbeck marble now?

These questions are answered in tomes on Dorset, embracing Purbeck as its jewel. Thus to avoid repetition this book is in the form of a discourse. In this manner it is hoped to turn a few of the more unusual stones.

I was born at Worth Matravers and my ancestors were islanders from at least 1539 (Dorset Tudor muster rolls), the same year as Henry VIII dissolved the monasteries. My grandfathers were in the stone trade. One owned quarries, the other was a monumental mason who followed the trade to Melbourne, where he worked on Government House, then to South Africa and North America.

Purbeck was a Royal Warren, favourite hunting ground for Kings. Thus the marble quarried was called King's marble. Marble, sensitive stuff, was the island's most prestigious export. The quarrymen themselves, called 'marblers', were a powerful if slightly eccentric workforce, with their ancient rights and customs.

Finally there was the utility of the place. Every day articles, from a house to a pigsty, a wall to a drinking trough, all of stone. Even bread bought with stone pennies and shillings weighing up to 144 lbs. Imagine that in your pocket! Yet walk carefully, the fields are on legs, what do you think holds up the Purbeck undergrounds? Purbeck is a unique place, where a stone might be just a stone, or ...?

Acknowledgements

My thanks to:

Terry Elson for his brilliant work with editing shears and tippex; Jeannie Elson for her insight and humanity; Mike Bizley with his 'walking to the gate' support; Sue Kendall for her directness and shaping from start to finish; photographer Toby Snazell for his persistence and expertise; photographer Gerald Corbett for his help, and for being in at the beginning; Clarence Payne for knowing where to look and what to look for; Alec Lander, an ever present fund of knowledge, which seems to increase with time; Rod Ivall for his steadfast proof-reading; Julian Cook for his superb free-hand drawing and the fun we had discussing them; Georgina Cook for her typing, consistency and heart-warming interest; Amberwood Graphics for their committed interest and understanding; my dear, courageous wife Wendy, for her support and good humour; my parents whose memories go back to a time when village life was a way of life; and to a host of people, too numerous to mention, who simply by giving their time encouraged me.

'The Articles' have been reproduced with kind permission from Hugh Jakes MA, County Archivist, Record Office, Dorchester, Dorset.

All rights reserved
No part of this publication may be reproduced, stored in a retrieval system, or transmitted, in any form or by any means without the prior permission in writing of the publisher, nor be otherwise circulated in any form of binding or cover other than that in which it is published and without a similar condition including this condition being imposed on the subsequent purchaser.

ISBN: 0 9517621 1 7

Published by:
David Pushman, Downsway, The Hyde, Langton Matravers, Dorset

Typesetting: Amberwood Graphics, Swanage, Dorset
Printing: Short Run Press Ltd, Exeter, Devon

Alec Lander

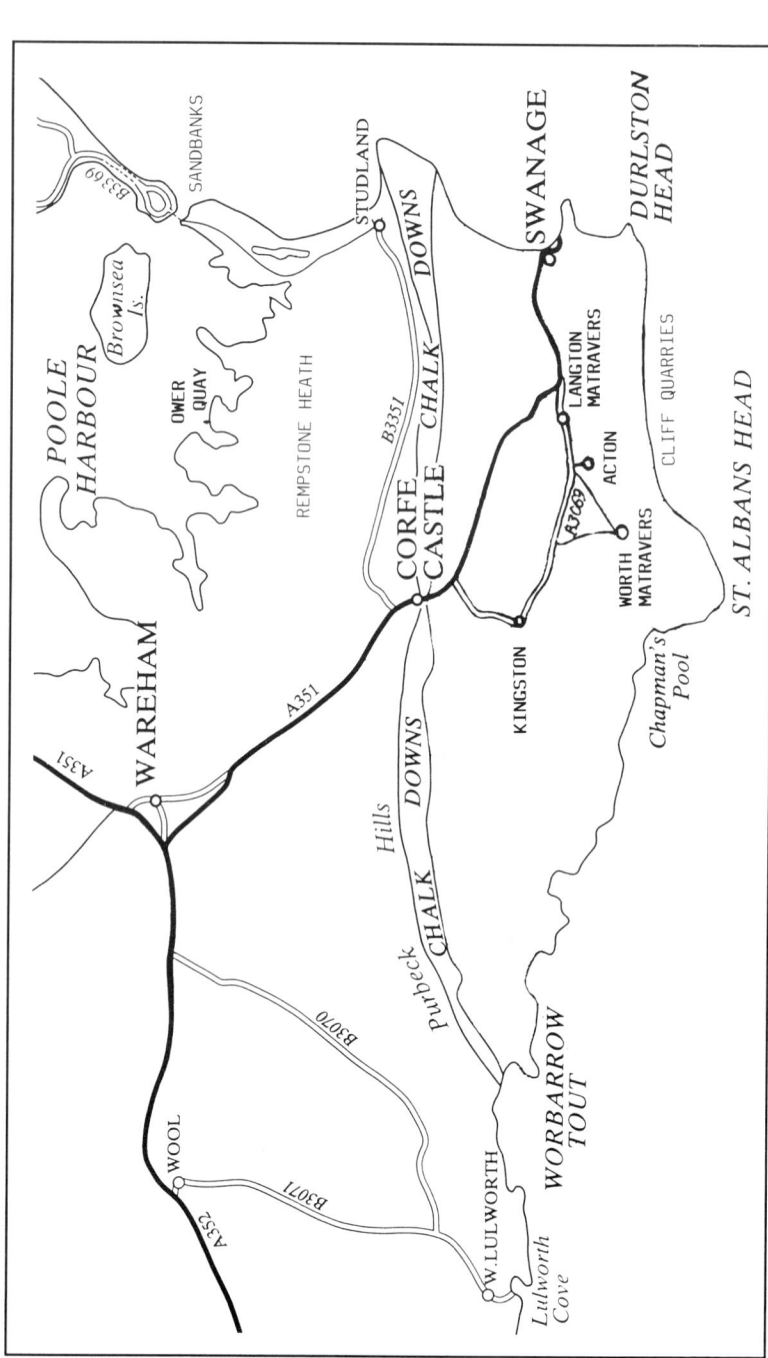

CONTENTS

INTRODUCTION

                                                                                       Page No.

Chapter 1	The Economics of Stone Quarrying	22
	The Charter	31
Chapter 2	Extraction and Transportation	34
Chapter 3	The Stone Shapes Land and Man	38
Chapter 4	Romance and Reality	51
	Suburban Simulation of Rural Reality	55
	The Future	59
The Articles		67
Addendum		74

PURBECK UNDERGROUND

Introduction

The title Purbeck Underground may suggest a movement, not of earth and stone, but of black chicanery ... undermining the fabric of society, like a war-time sapper. This would be a false impression. The book is not about subversion, but rather the ethos of the 'Island' over centuries of underground quarrying and china clay mining. Its workforce was a body of men more interested in their ancient rights than 'progress' or politics.

If you want their memorial look beneath you.

Today most incomers to Purbeck throttle hard across Wareham Bridge, heading like a pagan burial - due north to south, on to the open road (higher where it was once lower), twisting around the jagged ruins of Corfe Castle through to Swanage.
 The latter deserves a short description as it is the only town in the island.
 In the middle of the 19th century it was a stone port. Smelly cottages and shops built higgledy-piggledy, its inhabitants rough and ready for anything. But by the early part of the 20th century it had smartened itself up - was even called a 'family place'. Panama hats, furnished apartments, à la carte, en pension, churning paddle-steamers, tin buckets and spades. The Isle of Purbeck Toilet Club (for the old quarry hands?), bathing machines, Prep schools, a golf course (entrance fee 30/-), land in the choicest positions for sale, bedrooms from 2/6, breakfast 1/6, luncheon 2/- ....
 Purbeck has everything, newcomers exclaim ... and most of it on show. God made the Earth but squire grabbed most of it, is as true in Purbeck as anywhere else. Most of the estates are small with panoramic landscape - showing around contour and colour. There is also enormous mineral wealth, which today is extracted mechanically. A God-send to the labourer whose pay was not always commensurate to the hard, dirty

work done. A fact one can always bear in mind when touring Purbeck.

To introduce is to conduct into a place. Let us then ascend to a hill-top village, Kingston, 400 feet above sea level. Higher if you go to the top of Purbeck's cathedral tower.[1] From Kingston take the track to Swyre Head looking down on the Golden Bowl of Encombe, bounded by a blue white sea. Encombe, O.E. Henna Cumbra, 'fowls valley'. This land was until the Dissolution of the Monasteries owned by the Abbess of Shaftesbury. Kingston used often to be called Kingston Abbess. The 'Bowl' rises green and steep, and its rim is coloured purple with foxglove and heather. The area seemed always to have been pastoral ... of unenclosed sheep walks.

No man with blue-veined scars or shadow of a winding pit wheel ever fell across the vale of fowls.[2]

The Dissolution gave many of the smaller gentry a chance of power through land. It was at Encombe that die-hard Tory Lord Chancellor Eldon, holder of the Great Seal, lived in a great long, low house built by John Pitt. A mason might describe the house as a fine block job, the stones snug against each other, as if without mortar. His was a 'Show-Piece' estate and his powers were shown in getting and spending. Woe unto anyone who didn't understand that. A story runs, probably apocryphal, that the sudden dismissal of an estate farm manager followed his boast that he would ... 'make the farm pay'.

Peace Purbeck peace has often called men 'away from the Bar'. Why? Perhaps it was the ethos of Common Law. Castle and common side by side. An example exists at hand. From the Golden Bowl northward, there is a large area of common land leading down to Corfe Castle. The Right of Pasture, at four shillings per annum, of cutting wood, furze ... almost up to the castle walls.

In 1635 Sir John Bankes bought Corfe Castle. Attorney-General in 1634 and Chief Justice of the Common Pleas in 1640. 'A good man and true'. Also, I suspect, in Lord Acton's words - a man for peace at almost any price. Below the castle, along East Street, Sir John must have seen quarrymen chiselling off scars[3] that grew deeper under their feet than the foundations of his castle. Men belonging to a semi-religious trade guild - who

Open cast china clay mine - about 1920s

would be 'King's men' in times of danger.

Away from the stone country there were the china clay mining gentry. One mine owner told his clay diggers not to leave with boots caked with too much clay, for, if you leave with a piece as big as a sixpence ($2^1/_2$p) that is what it is worth, he said. One wonders how many men calculated their wages in buckets full of clay.[4] A great deal of Purbeck's working world was a 'different world' - secret, dark and dangerous.

Let us move on from 'Good Family' affairs - as a way of conducting into a place - and turn to Purbeck Proper.

To many people the name Purbeck is synonymous with the marble and stone trade. Up to about the middle of the 20th Century this wide-ranging industry was a working model of a loose-knit (part feudal) yet democratic community.

Richard Cobb, historian, wrote of a sense of place. A popular phrase now. Probably because we ourselves are at the end of a causeway over from Europe - today we don't really know our place. Formerly, place (though much of it 'common' place) meant ownership. Ownership is the land (power) question, on which buckets of ink and cruses of midnight oil have been spent. The best landowners *shared* the land. But for this to happen the right conditions had to be present, as in the forming of first life. The nearest Purbeck's working inhabitants came to sharing (themselves) was with their names, the quarries being mostly named after the quarrymen who worked them. This was further extended to masons who bore the names of places in quarrying areas, e.g. at Westminster in 1292 amongst the masons we find Edmond Corfe, Tom de Corfe, Hugo de Corfe and Peter Corf. There was a Pushman's Ware (quarry) somewhere at Durlston. In Purbeck there are many very old quarrying families. Older than the oldest records.

This then is the time to introduce myself. My surname is Pushman. Spelt variously as pushman, Puahman, Pushma, Pushmn, Poushman. One should remember that parish clerks wrote phonetically, and accents differed even from village to village. What one registrant mumbled another announced forcefully ... and the clerk scratched away, another name in the book. The first Pushman in the book of 'Births, Deaths and Marriages' at Swanage, beginning in the 16th century, was a George Pushman 'buryed', in 1577, ten years before Mary Queen of Scots was executed, and one year after Sir Christopher Hatton (then owner of Corfe Castle) was made Lord Chancellor. We were definitely in the stone trade in the 18th century, as a Henry Pushman (stone mason) was buried in Swanage in 1773.

The frontispiece in this book shows Thomas Pushman as witness to a HEADING OF A MANOR COURT ROLL dated 1720. This shows Thomas prepared to vouch, verify, testify, and give the benefit of his extensive local knowledge. He had a strong sense of place. One wonders what sort of place the next Pushman thought he was in. In the records of the 'Court Peculiar' of Corfe Castle the churchwardens once 'presented' John Pushman (and others) for playing in the churchyard on the Sabbath Day. Disreputable lad!

Family fortunes seldom continued in one stay. Today an overseer, tomorrow a recipient. This interdependence probably explains the nostalgic longing of British village pastoralists to see past rural life as communal and loving. Thomas Hardy observed more nearly when writing in 'The Return of the

Reproduced by the kindness of Mr. H. F. V. Johnstone of Poole, who adds that the only certainty about the spelling of Swanage was its uncertainty.

A copy of the books of the Court Roll

Native' of the Yeobright family who did not feel ... 'the necessity for preserving a friendly face towards men, bird and beast, which influenced their poorer neighbours'.

After the First World War a kind of social devolution appeared in 'pockets'. For instance in 1921 the village of Worth Matravers was sold to a draper. He sold it on to the villagers, so that nearly all owned their own homes. Thus Worth Matravers had no Squire, an Anglican vicar, who was a 'labour man', and a postmaster who was a Methodist.

Populist 'Purbeck man', whose name was half writ in water, of sea and quarry caves, cunning holes for brandy casks and Chinese tea, commandeered horses, surprised from their standing sleep, strong men, a long seaboard and dark nights.[5] Enough said; so much has been written before, except to say that smuggling was nasty, brutish and often short-lived, by hangman's rope or bullet.

This extract, written on vellum in a beautiful copperplate hand was found among the effects of 'Nurse' Pushman (local midwife) after she died. No one knows its provenance.

"*Barnabus Lowe, last of the preventative men of this section of the Dorset Coast. On one occasion he was waylayed by smugglers between Winspit and Seacombe and clubbed and left lying with his head over the cliff edge. Providentially found before regaining consciousness he was amongst the first in this locality to successfully undergo the operation trepanning, and lived to enjoy the peace of this village[6] to the ripe old age of 88. His epitaph, dated 3rd May 1891, in the nearby churchyard reads 'Behold the upright, for the end of that man is peace'.*"

Yet the hymn writer's encircling gloom was the pervasive climate of industrial England. In Purbeck, a green and airy land, quarrymen dressed mostly in black, smoked and chewed 'black man' tobacco, and descended down their black holes to work in a candlelit gloom that was air strangling and perpetually dangerous. Farm workers used tools of black iron heaviness and scullions black-leaded ranges and grates till they shone. Back at the loving villages the pervasion of darkness continued. Black widows, some merry, others sinister in their mourning clothes, 'fancy' men and women, 'natural' children, strong booze, foreign looking 'spies', tramps, the occasional suicide... and over all the dark oak stain of Victorian rectitude. In winter, church and chapel sent out light from their oil lamps. We, worshippers, wondered if ever a sailor thus warned, steered a course well seaward of their glow. Purbeck, by its smallness, close knitness, and variety, must pack in surprises. Hence, in the company of such simple thoughts, along perhaps the oldest inhabited seaboard in England, radar first performed its miracles, warning of raiders from the sky. Raiders on our own doorstep during the time it took to light a candle to bed.

Finally, on the Isle of Purbeck dinosaurs roamed. What type of creatures were they? Huge great behemoths, vanguards of a selfish gene society, gnashing their blood-clogged teeth, sharp-clawed and bellowing?

Today, we ask - keener than ever, has not the monster

another side? What was a tail waggle print a response to? Did the creatures scan the horizon for rain clouds, watch with saucer-sized eyes the night sky cascading with cinders? Did they not nuzzle their young? Those creatures in a new world. Now the world is captured by dinosaur mania, but is this not a paradox? When the old map-makers came to a country unexplored, they used to write - beyond this place there be dragons. In a sense of place, Purbeck, there were monsters. We have dinosaur DNA working inside the cells of our own bodies. Only connect.

'Beyond this place there be dragons'

Footnotes
1. Kingston's Early English Cathedral, built in 1880 by the 3rd Earl of Eldon - 'of very unusual sumptuousness'
2. Lord Eldon's father, William, was in the coal trade at Newcastle
3. 'Scars' - small pieces of chipped off marble or stone.
4. At the end of the nineteenth century over 70,000 tons of clay were dug from the claylands
5. Some quarrymen fished during the summer months
6. Worth Matravers

Chapter 1

THE ECONOMICS OF STONE QUARRYING

'There was something uncanny and underground about it all. It was an underworld. And quite incalculable.'
                                                                D.H. Lawrence

This discourse is mainly on Purbeck Marble, Purbeck Stone, China clay and those who dug it out.[1] Stone is now the prestige building material of the western world. Stone obliges tidiness and, wherever a person pulls down a tumbledown shack and builds in stone, he subscribes to a more tidy world. This is good for trade - the economic geology of Purbeck stone. Uniform walls, paths, garden ornaments ... and, if not a house of stone, at least a fireplace kit.

I will not attempt to write about the stratigraphy, tectonics, or palaeontology of the Isle of Purbeck. Firstly I am not qualified, and secondly, on this side of the apple pond we don't feel the desperate need to be factually informed about everything. Thus, this discourse will be aberrant like stone strata - which seldom run in a straight line.

To know that the Romans were here in Purbeck may give the reader a frisson. Roman coins, bones, skulls, shale artefacts, share common ground with pagan superstition. The Harp Stone, erect in a hedgerow, Agglestone; like a dead beetle on its back; little Puck Stone (Goblin Stone), and yet further back - whilst sleepy dust held the world in twilight - marks where the dinosaur ran and freshwater snails crowded together to form Purbeck marble.

Before I write on, I will define the stuff I am writing about. The dictionary definition of stone runs from the matter of which rocks consist, to a slang word for testicle. Purbeck Stone (of seventy beds) is over all durable and drab coloured. Most Middle Purbeck stone improves with age. It weathers well and, splashed with lichen, blends with almost any background. The building stones which occur in the Middle Purbeck are quarried mainly south west of Swanage, at Herston and Acton. Acton particularly is riddled with old 'undergrounds' and is a good example of the difference between a large mine or open-cast working with a mine owner, and a quarr[2] hole no larger than a large well. No owner could 'lock out' that type of independent work force.

Along the cliffs, the stone is known as Purbeck Portland. The stone was quarried by means of galleries driven into the face of the cliff or into the sides of the dug coombs, which descended to the sea at Anvil Point, Seacombe, and Winspit. These 'caves' are interesting because they were not only quarried for stone but were favourite smugglers' resorts, a haunt against the press gang, and a good roof for hermits.

It was ironic that an island race that exported tens of thousands of tons of stone should itself be so poorly housed. Almost Steinbeckian in its galvanised iron huts, its 'tin bath' poverty, dust, mud and ramshackle vehicles. There are several old chestnuts, hardened into conkers, that do the rounds when anyone writes about the stone industry in Purbeck. Most anecdotes end with the story, a few compel us to 'think on'. One story that compels a 'think on' is of a quarry man who used to look at his children's faces by the light of a candle before he went to work - in case he never saw them again.

Underground quarrying was dangerous work. As well as being physically strong, a quarryman had to be psychologically strong. The sensory deprivation would have driven many men insane, but quarrymen were almost casual about danger. Imagine one hundred feet below the surface wresting a huge stone with little paddles, often only a little longer than a poker - a stone that could twist or fall without warning - all this in a very confined space, by the dim light of a candle. Perpetual twilight was their working environment. In winter, quarrymen rarely saw the sun. Walking to work, all day underground, walking home, all in dusk and darkness. Many were the ways of dark dealing when a stone became a thing of value, especially between quarryman and merchant. This probably occurred because a stone was handled so many times. Some merchants operated the truck system - a mountain of stone for a pat of butter.

This 'company store' policy kept most quarrymen in perpetual debt for, although the quarrymen met every Shrove Tuesday to fix their prices, this system was not flexible enough to counter the traders' ability to raise food prices at a stroke.

To forestall this exploitation of workers the Truck Acts were passed in Parliament in 1831, 1896 and 1970, to prevent employers misusing wage payment systems to the detriment of their workers. The broad effect of the Truck Acts was to force employers to pay employees in coins of the realm.

Every trade has its tricks, its knack of doing things, its secrets. Some are practical - like walking a stone, or lifting without lumping your entrails through your belly. Other tricks concerned the mason at his desk. There was a method of cubing stone used by the 'old hands'. It was a small scale calculus called little inches, whether anyone today knows the system is doubtful. Many trade secrets were lost ... 'beyond time where memory runneth', as well as a whole empire of 'footprints' and a vast quantity of Purbeck marble (destroyed mostly by Henry VIII), and a Purbeck Marblers' Charter ... lost? Finally, one wonders how much talent was lost, particularly artistic talent, cutting, shaping, finishing that produced fabric beauty and artefact attraction. Much has always been expected of the skilled artisan. Dictionary definition of the word artisan:- Latin: artitus - skilled, ars, artis - art. But, after the last stone was laid, the craftsmen disappeared, in some cultures for ever. Perhaps, to obviate this, most crafts brothers dismissed their work as - just another job.

All things work together for the great and the good. Though in war the 'brother' reappears. It seems that neither principalities nor powers (of stone) can separate the artisan from the call of war. At the call he has to surrender tool and tythe for bayonet and bullet. Quarrymen must have felt the trenches less alien than most men, exchanging a 'lane' for a dug out ... and, after it was all over, the loneliness of a survivor ... Poor Tommy ... a face among skulls. The uses of stone were many in both World Wars, especially the second. It is beyond the scope of this discourse to try to turn every stone. Times had changed and a chance remark of one quarry owner to another (post Second World War) illustrates this. First quarryman, "we won't have them back like this, Jack as good as his master". Second quarry owner, "don't worry, they won't want to come back".

But let us dive into the maelstrom of time to consider events of cosmic significance. Over the past few hundred million years a kilometre-sized body must have struck the Earth, on average, once every million years or so, and an object of ten kilometres every fifty to a hundred million years. As this impact occurred on Earth, it would have thrown hundreds of millions of tons of dust into the atmosphere, leaving a world that existed in a perpetual twilight, a proto-nuclear winter. It is possible that seventy million years ago such an event occurred, causing a sudden major extinction of species, including dinosaurs who had populated the planet for one hundred and thirty million years. But their Herculean presence was such that they would not be dismissed without leaving evidence of their tenure.

Now conjure a transposition to one hundred years ago! In candle-light, a quarryman is digging a bed of stone and notices it suddenly begins to dip down and then breaks into irregular shapes. "Damn," he whispers, "Boils." He throws them over in disgust and works on till he comes to a level bed again. He did not know that he had touched the bottom of a watering hole in Darkest Purbeck. In this way, more footprints were broken up than are likely to be found in the future. These footprints are found mainly in the roach stratum, though many beds had the right kind of emollience - gypsum for instance, often called the plaster bed, for making plaster of Paris[3]. Sometimes other fossils were found, fossilised skin, an impression of a tail. Maybe some of these creatures were more reptilian than we think, sized from a bootlace to a bus. Little is known for sure. Not many experts would go to the stake on 'facts'. After all, science is often only a matter of updating theories.

By the early nineteen-fifties, few men worked underground. The 'dozer' had replaced pick and shovel, and stone was in demand. Men looked after themselves. After the Second World War the stone industry needed a buzz-word, a logo ... it got it, a footprint. This phenomenon came running out of the rock. A general and increasing interest in fossils was a 'hand me down' from the Victorian gentry. What they couldn't stuff they still collected.

A dug-out wine cellar produced dozens of Viking bones (most of them 'huge fellows'). Fragile little bones were under glass, on yellowing cotton wool ... But the new fossil folk wanted their bones outside - on a house or garden wall - for everybody to see. Thus, a demand was created and the market responded. Related conversation of spiv and quarryman: Spiv, "Have you got a really good footprint guv'nor? You know the business, I will pay good money for it." Quarryman, "What do you want it for?" Spiv, "To use as a cast - to make concrete footprints." No wonder the same quarryman, when he cracked open a stone and found water, drank it himself.

I must stir the sand in this arena - of man and only man begot. It has been said that building a house is a provocative act. If this is true, then quarrymen provide the provocative material and even the afore-written-about fossil embellishments - set forever in stone. This need to exhibit a fossil path goes beyond mere prettification, it touches bedrock bottom. Was this because early 'bone merchants' thought of formed stones in terms of very big men rather than animals? To substantiate this idea, there were giants of legend and, through recordable history, huge men in the earth, many between seven feet and nine feet tall. To better illustrate this formed stone idea and how men unconsciously sought verification in the belief that all shapes were as in Adam, may I quote from the writings of a Professor Plott.

In 1677 Robert Plott (Professor of Chemistry at Oxford University) published a book, 'The Natural History of Oxford', in which he describes a massive thigh bone dug up at Carnwall, Oxfordshire. It was almost certainly from a megalosaurus. Plott was unaware of the significance of his find, which he describes in a chapter on 'Of formed stones'. Now the plot thickens. In a later edition of his work - due to an editorial error - the fragment was wrongly labelled scrotum humanum (man's scrotum), and type of formed stone. Plott actually believed that a man had existed with a 20lb scrotum, two feet around. But one should not find this incredible when one considers the Cerne Abbas Giant, of 'spirited design' with a performance organ of 22 feet. Bottle and balls, homes built of stone, rockery gardens, buck giants, quarrymen of brute strength, quarry work called 'savage amusement'.

We will now discuss in a little more pragmatic detail, stone quarrying and its transportation.

Hutchins says that Corfe Castle is the principal and only town in the Island - and the parish is very extensive. Thus, we can warily surmise that stone was quarried from the west, eastward, and 'outcrops' from north to south. From the top beds to the bottom bed of usable stone - the new vein.

Who named the beds of stone? First, it must have been the quarrymen, who would have named them from their usability or character. 'He that works with stone must share its nature.' Brassy Bed, Sad Bed, Dun Cow, Tombstone, ... we need to put a preservation order on these names and how they were pronounced. Local words lost are lost for ever. More modernly, geologists went by the texture of stone when naming beds. Rag Bed, for instance, they called Beef Bed, a grainy cut of beef - some quarrymen capped this by calling 'Rag' the Bully Beef Bed. This sentiment - that the old ways and words should be preserved to speak for themselves - is the keystone of this discourse.

What of the stuff itself - the stone? When it had been man-handled, dressed, or finely masoned - what then? 'What then' is what most writing about stone is about. 'The trade of this Island consists in stone dug here (Corfe Castle) and exported formerly from Ower Quay but now wholly at Swanage.'

In terms of archaeology, Ower Quay is not old. It is newly old yet not an upright stone remains. Milton Abbey once held Ora or Ower, and, at the time of Edward the Confessor, it was taxed at three hides. Little is known about the size of the quay or its construction. A few stones of mixed strata, sandstone to Purbeck marble, have been found. Pin-pointing a former sea site is difficult, time and tide are your reckoners. For, as well as the 'heavy stage' quay, there were landing stages along the shore, rotted away, plank by plank.

Of great importance to this discourse is that Ower was the principal port for transporting stone out of Purbeck. Loading must have been done in the traditional way. There is evidence that 'sea horses' were stabled near Cleavil Point. Passage wise, the horses would have dragged their loads of stone along the quay to the waiting barges. It is possible that some loads were 'carted' into the sea, as at Swanage, but deep soft mud would have made this hazardous. Once the stone was secured on a barge it was rowed out to the deep draught vessels anchored off shore. That man-handling, horse and wind power, was how, reader, stone and marble was transported from a remote isle off the Dorset coast to the Great Wen, waterside cities and towns.

Ower's heyday was when Corfe Castle was under construction, it was the seaport of a bustling trade route. Heavy commodities, timber, iron ... were waggoned across the heath. It is said that vestiges of the old route still remain. In winter, it must have been a quag of a journey. Wind and rain sheeting across the open heath. But in summer, in gridiron heat one might imagine it worse. The true heath hunters are its insects, wasps, bees, deer flies, shimmer the air with their number, and thunder gnats quarter closely every inch of sweat-laced skin ... what a life for man and beast.

The construction, finding a bottom, of a dry roadway must have been difficult. Much of the heath is bog land. Bogs are sinister, waitful places. A sea yields a catch though taking lives, most of nature is sowable and reapable ... but not a bog. The predominant flora is gorse, mile upon mile of sight searing

Ower Quay looking out towards the south deep channel

gorse. The carters and 'stone men' must have seen yellow for days after a journey. Were the men who took the stone to Ower Quay quarrymen or carters? Maybe they were a mixture breed of élite journeying men knowing much about stone and horses.

Leaving Corfe, a quite cosmopolitan small town under the great castle, for a remote backwater must have been very de-trop. Though, at journey's end, the journeying man seemed to have stayed long enough to get skull-less on fine ale. For once there, it was Shrove Tuesday every day. Why? Because the charming house now standing within inches of high tide was then an ale house ... without a name. For the home-brewed beer, two pecks of malt and half a pound of hops were used for a single brewing. If the traveller was a sporting man did he stay long enough to bag a few ducks or a goose? ... for the area teems with bird life.

This is a wild fringe of Wessex where turf and timber preceded stone and mortar. It is a wide open sea meadow where waders feed and primp, flat-fish scuttle sand and wise-eyed swans circle in the mist. Ducks apart, ale and stone link 'Ower and Ower', which might be said to bring us to Shrove Tuesday proper. The Ancient Order of Purbeck Marblers and Stone Cutters', Shrove Tuesday and Ash Wednesday traditions and shindigs must be known in Dorset and wherever stone is quarried.

To go into detail is not possible - the Orders' rituals are secret. However these shindigs always ended in a journey - the tribute of pepper to Ower quay. The track to Ower seemed almost a gnomon to the Stone trade. As afore written it was lonely and long.

To begin the long journey loads of stone would leave the area of Worth, Langton, Acton, to be carted down a steep lane, Court Pound, Afflington, (Crack) Lane, (Primrose Hill), Haycrafts Lane, to 'middle around' Scowles then across the common to Corfe. These lanes seem hardly to have silenced the grinding of the cart wheels, and the horses shoes polished on the pearl white downsvein[4]. Avoidance of 'up hill' would have been a quarriers' first thought when planning a route. From Corfe Castle, across the open land of Rempstone Heath to Ower was a straight line, hardly a mole hill.

A question any reader might ask is why trundle stone half way around Purbeck when you have a good port on your doorstep, downhill nearly all the way to Swanage? Why is a good question, because no one can answer it. Swanage quarrymen were bred for their trade, hard work breeds hard men. Many called themselves East County men, everybody else was a West County man. Many 'old hands' spoke of a feud between East and West County men. Might it not have been too dangerous for Langton men to attempt a journey through to Swanage? They would have felt trapped, and once there almost waiting for the waters of the bay to close over them. A watery grave and a lost cart of stone. One has to imagine such a scenario, there are few records about quarrymens' feelings, only what they did with hammer in one hand and punch[5] in the other.

The business of the movement of stone had almost everything to do with the slump that followed the Civil War. If Swanage was out of bounds, how could carts of stone still get through to Ower? W.H. Hardy in 'Old Swanage and Purbeck' says - "Very soon after the Castle was besieged and demolished, and the roads rendered impossible by the hundreds of tons of rubbish which were precipitated into the valley from the ruins of Corfe Castle." One can assume that for a period the roadways were blocked, although stone traffic, around the old paths continued right up to the beginning of the 18th century. More about this later.

Footnote
1. Discourse: dis - a name for Pluto, hence the infernal world (underground)
course - a range of stones on the same level in building.
2. Local dialect word for quarry.
3. About 1895 marble was quarried south-west of Orchard for making cement.
4. Downsvein: vein of stone.
5. Basic masonry tool used for removing waste stone.

THE CHARTER

Whilst path-finding we cannot rush on without a word about the conundrum of a Purbeck Marblers' and Stone Cutter's Charter. It was said this charter gave the quarrymen the right to open an underground quarry where they liked, on anyone's land, provided they paid the Royalties on the stone taken to the landowner. An outsider (Purbeckians have got used to it) might think this almost too good to be true. Thus we need an 'Overburden'[1] of proof.

Trying to trace the Charter is elusive work. It seem to lie somewhere between the Land of Nod and a wink. A quarryman from Derbyshire might ask, 'Did scrivener, quill and parchment come together, does a document exist?' If it once did and has slipped through time's misty fingers, what happened to it? Locally, no one seems to know and it is right to state that no archivist has any record of this Charter. Progressively, the next logical question is - who were those said to have granted a Charter? Henry III's name is tossed around like a Shrove Tuesday pancake. History tells us he granted a market and fair at Afflington, as at Corfe. Costless favours from marble-hearted Henry. Anyway, the very word Charter would have stuck in his throat. For the Great Charter that King John rolled on the floor biting reeds after signing, was in no greater favour with his son. Changeable, misruler, wrester of rights (not signatory), religious, bad-tempered ... a man likely to grant a Charter?

For some inexplicable reason, Queen Anne[2] lived in the minds of some quarrymen. Queen Anne, bountiful to clergymen, a rank Tory, who loved law and order as much as best brandy, who gave her name to so many things from a fan to a footstool, but not, I suspect, a Marbler's Charter[3]. Though there are exceptions to every Royal rule. Here is one:-

In the 18th century, the ecclesiastical fabric of London began to rise again. In this sense only was Queen Anne involved with quarrymen. Thus in 1703 she granted an Order to Christopher Wren allowing stone to leave Portland only by licence. Portland quarries railed at this, for they had 'beyond the memory of man raised stone by custom and exported such stone at pleasure without licence...', Purbeck with its paving stone, Portland with its prestige stone, by custom to the cities and towns. (The Portland Island Stone Grant was renewed by Queen Anne in 1708).

Since this lapses into Royal 'stick-a-Jousting-Pin-time', how about that chance-comer Charles Stuart? After fleeing the Battle of Worcester, 'Dorset' hid him well, in secret rooms and green trees; ending in a last step from back alley Poole onto a small coal brig across the English Channel to France. Later as Charles II[4], he knew Purbeck as an important area to be defended. More importantly, he needed to settle the nation down. London had to be rebuilt after the Great Fire, the marble trade was in terminal decline and the new 'undergrounds' were soon to open up. What better time to grant a Charter?[5]

Finally in that era the socio-religious 'lanes' were not of doubt but of sureness and certainty. Many 'old-time' quarrymen honestly believed that a Charter had been granted and it was in that belief that they had been thought worthy, that the 'spirit' of a Charter should continue traditionally as long as stone is quarried in Purbeck.

Historically, it seems likely that 'something' happened. Some kind of Charter, length of parchment, written in dog Latin, a blob of wax, granted perhaps for sea defence work. An island race must always have eyes 'out to sea'. Courage would be there, as in the last war when a Home Guard quarryman ran with his shovel at some Americans on a coastal exercise - shouting, 'Be you German? Be you French? ... Be you the enemy?'

This independence widened inter-relationship. Transport, advertising, offices, technology - the whole shebang of modern quarrying. It also allows a backward looking honesty without too much veneration for the past. The mason was often imbued with a kind of holiness that he neither deserved nor needed. Theology joining with geology for once.

Writers, historians, write of the mason's signature or mark on a cathedral or great building, but a lot of mediaeval stone - work fell down, only the best is standing. Parts of many glorious cathedrals were jerry-built. Torture chambers and dungeons were also a product of the mason's craft.

*'Like him of whom the poet sings, a mason, I
Tame the wild stones to make a jail'*

Many of the human race made themselves miserable and anguished over stone. A large stone was often the pagan altar for human sacrifice - hag stones were hung around the necks against witches ... the evil eye ...

Stone capstan!

Footnotes
1. Overburden: top soil that has to be cleared before the stone beds are reached
2. Further research suggests this was a derogatory term (origin unknown) used by some outside the (closed Purbeck Shop) stone trade for those in it. The term 'Queen Anne' was and still is, given to quarrymen by people outside the trade
3. Most men who had not obtained sanction for their associations before the Black Death were not likely to obtain it easily afterwards
4. No monarch was more a deceiver of observers of his own day and historians of our own. (Richard Green, History of the English People)
5. Not to be confused with the Charter granted by King Charles II to the borough of Corfe confirming the same privileges to Sir John Bankes and his heirs as Queen Elizabeth granted to Lord of the Manor Sir Christopher Hatton.

Chapter 2

EXTRACTION AND TRANSPORTATION

I want this discourse to be balanced ... a look, not only at the cleared-up façade but round the back, and up along where the pigeons murmur among the melting faceless saints.

Thus, into the oft-picked-over boney[1] carcase we grope.

Purbeck is not broken but cracked off from the main by a trickling stream. It is mainly stonecutters' country - with some lowland heath. Like an old rotten borough, its 'capital' is a ruin. Corfe Castle was a busy place and the very early and mediaeval centre of the Purbeck stone trade. The town's wide streets must have rung with the sound of hammer and punch, mallet and chisel. We know the Romans were here, quarrying for marble, yet they have left little evidence. It's a pity the clerk was not thought worthy of his hire, without scrip one has to fall back on imagination, one can imagine a Roman quarryman digging for the thin bed of Purbeck marble in a dank valley on a cold hillside. How he must have longed for the blue of a Mediterranean sky. But he was not alone in his misery. The upland lawns of Purbeck have a soft almost green powdery light. Yet below there exists the man-made darkness of the underground quarries. These began in the 18th century. Men dug down, like well sinkers, and then hit along into the living stone. Some quarries had a good ceiling, the quarriers could stand, others were narrow seamed (as low as three feet), claustrophobic, air strangling, tricked up on narrow little 'legs' and illumined by clay held candles.[2] The undergrounds were uncharted places - a warren of tunnels. Sometimes they collapsed, often lives were lost, bad accidents were common, and a house built over an underground had not always a firm foundation.

On passing a deep brown hole, an explorer to the area might think it a monster's lair - especially on a frosty morning with steam issuing from the depths. But in truth these were dens of cruelly worked men. 'Needs must' work. In a museum at Corfe Castle there is exhibited a huge saw, once used by two work-men. Its big teeth were well spaced, and it must have taken tremendous strength, as well as co-ordination, to move it an inch. Underneath is printed on a card - 'Man Killer. Roach-Belly Cross-Cut Saw.'

Employment in the china clay mines, that part of the Island where stone gives way to lowland heath, in the stone quarries, and all the allied trades, was man killing work. If work didn't kill it often maimed. Men with protruding ruptures, near under the skin like bat wing bones, limbs twisted as with disease, hands broken into deep chaps, into which they rubbed cobblers' wax .... Examining old underground workings the explorer will sometimes find an iron spike driven into the gallery wall. These had no constructional use, they merely marked the place where a quarryman had died: the nobility of hard labour?

Yet all that graft went unrecorded until the early 19th century, when recording agents appeared. These agents, artists, photographers, writers, theatricals, were fascinated by what they found. 'Locals', many of whom were in their villages when Corfe had its castle, going to sea in bowler hats, underground in moleskin trousers, wedded to women, patched up and hard handed (from manual work), and hermits cooking and sleeping in quarry caves. Unfortunately, the recorder seldom 'belonged' - so cause and context were often overlooked. As ever the 'local' was gibbeted with the artist. The artist who slithered into his defence chain mail at the first sight of a poor old truth. There are many developed reasons for this, some almost surreal.[3] Now to more back braking work, transporting stone down hill to Swanage.

There is no better way I can describe this transportation than by quoting from Hutchins. "If we were to take our minds back to the 1850s, 1860s, and glance at the east end of the town from the Royal Victoria Hotel around the shore to the White House, our eyes would be struck by the immense piles of stone on the 'bankers', amounting to thousands of tons, stacked ready for shipment, while, in the narrow streets and road to the quarries, would be seen a continuous line of stone waggons and carts, either returning empty or bringing fresh supplies of stone from the seemingly inexhaustible quarries. During the fine hot weather of summer, the almost ceaseless grinding of those heavily laden vehicles would crush the roads to powder, and, when the wind rose, the dust would be suffocating, while, in the winter, the mud on the roads would be inches deep, making them almost impassable by foot passengers". (So Hutchins writes, and this reader was the easy route!)

Since Purbeck is an island and exports mainly itself (mineral wealth), transportation has always been a problem, especially in the early years. Stone had to be rolled, by wagon wheel or roller, dragged by sledge, or even carried across the backs of some quarriers.

Transportation of stone in Durlston Bay was shipped in a different way. They used a strong ladder with one end on the beach and the other on the boat, with a man on each side of the ladder breast high in the water, rolling the stones into the waiting boat.

I want to describe, as a hat would describe a head, an imaginary journey of a single stone from say, Acton Common to Swanage. A big thornback weighing over a ton. It had been difficult to 'paddle' out, one corner had seemed to nib over into a groove. The quarry floor was sticky yellow, and the candle's flame blackened the low ceiling. Sweating stubbled faces inspected the problem - a swig of cold tea, one more great effort and it was free. A big stone, grey-blue as a crab's shell, lifted on to a low cart, chained firm and winched to the surface by a sour-faced donkey. There to be 'cut up' and 'punched off' into the shape of a two foot kerb. Thence to be loaded on to a sturdy waggon and dragged and braked to Swanage, with all the attendant perils of a huge load, and at last to a maze of bankers, where unloaded, the thornback, in the plural of many hundred weights, would await onward shipment. Finally, its turn came, and it would be loaded on to the ships either from the stone quay or on to stone carts, pulled by horses on the narrow-gauge railway that led out to the old pier and thence onto the waiting ships. Or it could have a more tortuous journey where it was loaded on to a bier-like cart with huge wheels and drawn by horses into the sea, the blue sea again, where, from under its sub-tropical warmth, it formed its awkward shape. Further cursed and struggled on to barges and rowed out to the stone ships, with their coloured sails and sea scoured anchors, straining and ready like sea horses to race around the coast - to be unloaded and finally set at the edge of some suburban pavement. It was for this that quarrymen, sailors, loaders, grunted, sweated, daily endangering their lives for pitiful pittance wages. But then we have read somewhere before about what was expected of the brute, the slave in Victorian England. All this until the coming of the railway into Swanage in 1885 (when the quarrymen and their wives turned up with shovels to kill the 'hissing monster', which they considered was the work of the devil!).

Today, stone is transported in high-powered lorries, with cabs as comfortable as a driver's front room. All this powered movement began after the First World War with solid tyred chain driven lorries. Names to make the old-time drivers shudder along their spines: Liberty, Peerless, Packard, Thornycroft, Renault, Leyland... all chugging out of Purbeck at the regulation 16 m.p.h., or, with a following wind and a great struggle, 30 m.p.h. But occasionally, even then, an odd brute of a stone won the day to stay at home ... scorning prose, a quarryman would have none of it. An example of the 'stay at homes' can be seen at Seacombe Valley, where a few large stones are beside the track. That was where a driver had one too heavy on board ... and had to bar it off.

Footnotes
1. boney: a local name for stony
2. These candles were long and thin, sold 16 to the pound, and supplied by a firm named Price.
3. In the early years of the 20th century many 'artists' perigrinated to Purbeck, squiring third rate actresses, driving low slung sports cars, bellying up to snug room bars... Word had reached the Metropolis that a fairy land existed of exquisites in red velvet hats, posers in cowls and black cloaks, near naked nymphs cavorting around blue pools, natural children, brown and muddy, stickle jar-ed... the unconscious freed in a splattering of oils. Whilst underneath - to round off the players, quarriers, nightsighted, primitive, cramped, had no such freedom to be recorded. The modern artist with his battery of equipment 'sees all men as they really are', the miasma has lifted.

Chapter 3

THE STONE SHAPES LAND AND MAN

If an island could speak in the Classic heroic tradition - as a god in the bower tresses of the stars - I am sure it would ask why? For, like Prometheus, its innards yet taken - go on renewing themselves unseen. For no eye hath seen the stone before it is quarried, nor the oil before it gushed, nor the snaking seams of china clay. All was closed over since the planet Earth laid down her treasures.

'Humanity appears upon the scene, hand in hand with trouble.' The idea of a contented people in a paradise garden abuts against what we know of mankind's 'state of nature'. True-seeming it is more a condition of war, of everyone against everyone. One might even consider any kind of building work a compounding of this condition. Unwitting palpability, for one stone upon another is a challenge, whilst a pile is a definite declaration of war. How does this condition (of war) manifest itself? First, Britain's heritage - is not a great part of it thrown down ruins? Second, a mason's work is mainly enclosing space. Thus when space has been enclosed for a very long time, some people can sense an atmosphere, as though the stones are speaking. If Corfe Castle's spaces could speak, they would tell of black deeds, plotted and in cold blood ... as well as pageantry and gallantry.

What of other 'atmospheric' buildings? 'Conscious fabric'? From the 11th to the 15th Century many religious houses were built. Religion (a good customer) had to have a roof over its head. Nearly all, especially in the South of England, contained Purbeck marble. From city cathedral to abbeys 'in remote and not populous places', to countless parish churches, *viviparus*[1] adorns and decorates. Purbeck marble insists on its nature. Though heavy and tough to work, it is delicate stuff and bruises with ill use. It is also fussy about where it belongs. Built as outside fabric it flakes and goes dull as an old gun barrel. But not everyone loved temples of sparkle and polish. To the Puritans it was anathema. Oliver Cromwell would have seen the flaking and dulling as an Act of God.

Oliver Cromwell's great urgency to be done and moving before all his dreams crumbled to dust affected the stone trade in Purbeck. By slighting the castle walls, he rendered it unsafe to walk near and, more importantly, the hundreds of tons of fallen masonry made the roads around impassable. The portage area of Wareham became almost a peninsula.

Thus, by the end of the 17th Century, the majority of stonemasons left from Corfe, eastward to Swanage. One 'knock-on' effect of the Civil War. But before leaving, let us imagine the old sounds around Corfe. This area of east west Purbeck must have been a far more clamorous place then. The Romans, with their foreign tongue and intimacy with marble; carters, with their deep guttural dialect, boys blowing horns to warn of the approach of a stone cart. Noise, dust, and mud, all to do with the stone trade, which must have extended over most of the Island.

One suspects that as quarrymen moved into the downland area of the east of Worth, Acton Common, Langton Matravers, and Swanage, so they made more ridding waste. As well, the bulk of stone quarried was left in heaps in the spring and summer to allow it to 'weather'. Most of the quarry land was owned by the Bankes family, and their traditions lead back to Corfe, its castle, and the whole hotchpotch of hot cinders, stones, ancient rights, ordnance, boiling oil ... Friend, grub down lower.

When a quarry is 'worked out' or exhausted, this is what a quarryman has to do to open a new quarry. The quarrier applies to the proprietor of the land (through an agent) for leave to open quarry, and, if he consents and the quarrier opens the ground and finds stone there, he claims the exclusive privilege and use of the new quarry, paying the proprietor of the land the customary acknowledgements for the different sorts of stone, and, by the custom of the Island, such exclusive right is lost to the quarrier if he deserts the quarry or leaves it unworked for a year and a day. This is a reasonable tie up on the quarrier to work his quarry with effort, and a security that the proprietor

Stones Weathering — M. Bizley

of the land shall have the customary acknowledgements for every foot or ton of stone found there - which is his only compensation for the unavoidable damage done to his land.

Such an agreement as that would have been drawn up between Bankes Estate and the quarrier. At this point, it is interesting to compare one proprietor with another, especially when they are juxtaposed. Proprietor Bankes took a lot of stick - and generally showed remarkable forbearance. Lord Eldon didn't put himself within range of a stick. At Kingston, on the Earl's estate, the stone was quarried and worked by his own men for the estate only. There are thousands of tons of good stone under Kingston village. As old families, the Bankes were defending the Royalist cause before the Earl of Eldon's ancestors touched their first knob of coal. Thus, the power of political intrigue and social status burned bright in them.

One such intrigue was the mysterious architectural pile of burr stone and marble designed by G. E. Street at a cost of sixty thousand pounds. The church, Early English in style, with its

Edmund Burke and Lord Eldon daily proclaimed their aversion to progress of every sort

'Purbeck Cathedral' (Kingston)

tower, is a symbolic landmark that dominates the landscape. Built to whose glory? Why was it built? The estate already had a church - meagre looking but respectable enough, and the Wesleyans had their little place at the bottom of the hill. Was it defensive philanthropy - to keep quarrymen working through a lean time, or was it the long cold shadow of an old fear, of blade and blood, of the extinction of their order? The 1st Earl of Eldon lived in terror (with many of his ilk) of anything that smacked of the French Revolution. The 3rd Earl saw about him signs of great social unrest - throughout the country. Powerful and 'next door' were a band of strong men with little to do except to go underground and plot. To compound the threat - in the 1880s there was a bad recession in the stone trade.

Work on the church was begun in 1880. It was said by some quarrymen that the work was too easy, so easy that many men used to work by day on the church and go home in the evening so fresh that they would go to work in their quarries. When the church was finished the stone trade continued to slump and the quarrymen blamed the estate for taking them away from working in their own quarries - as men might if they had been deceived by a soft option. But the 'county seats' remained and the revolutioneers' blade and resolution finally rusted out. Fear, for the moment, would recede ... paradoxically due to what they feared. Maybe this is a rather imaginative interpretation of things seen, but motives lie deep, deeper than many a foundation stone.

But I am ahead of my discourse. Let us go to a quarryman's cottage - the area we were around. What was it like? Probably a mean dwelling built in the 18th or 19th century - of local stone, with wood, maybe locally beachcombed - the beach being a good source of free timber. Its total cost would have been but a few pounds. Would you like to see inside? Before you enter, you might like to wipe your shoes ... on a few damp sack bags, which if you turn over, will be almost entirely made up of pink wriggling worms. Inside, the atmosphere would probably be fetid, especially in winter, with quarry clothes to dry. The ceiling is low, as are the 'bull's eye' windows. Children, curious as monkeys, half starved, often badly dressed, hanging on to their mother's skirt for security. Many won't survive the season they are living in. Earlier cottage dwellers would have had an open fire, often of driftwood, which, salt-encrusted, would spit and pop, blue-flamed, up the soot shivering chimney. Later generations would have to survive the foul smoking Valor stove upon which a lot of cooking was done. Food was more messy (stews) than meaty. Meat, unless half a pig, was often the result of a well-aimed stone at a rabbit, or a cleverly set snare. Fish was comparatively cheap; shellfish, especially crabs, almost given away, and fresh herrings from Swanage Bay one penny each or thirteen for a shilling. How popular was the halfpenny - 'half a penny's worth of milk please and plenty for the cat'. Vegetables were plentiful, thanks to the thunder bucket. The soil was like thick loamy black sand - it ran cool through your fingers. One man said he grew leeks as big around as a donkey's cock, and his cabbages could only be taken home in a horse-drawn dung pot. What food a quarryman went to work on is boring, you will exclaim, but the First World War was won on bully beef and hard tack biscuits. At night, our cottage family would sleep head to toe - covered with a smudged, grease grey eiderdown. Mice would muscle and scuttle for the odd crumb. A quarrier's coat, dried hard over a chair, would suddenly fall forward - as if even clothes are always crouched in toil. A sleeper, usurped of a corner of the blanket, will clutch around - and quickly turn over in angry sleep.

Looking back at the postwar period of the 1930s, it is interesting to note that, as mass production increased, household appliances, modern furniture, the magic of electricity - so the old-fashioned 'comfort objects', single and double brass paraffin lamps, 'pan pipes' bedheads, warming pans (still in use), were the first to be thrown over cliffs and down old quarry holes.

What of the quarrymen themselves? Who portrayed them? Men by nature equal, Thomas Hobbes said. Their short straw had been an unlucky one - the dangerous and brutally hard life of a quarryman. Sometimes a spawl in just the right place in a thin pillar kept Atlas there - holding the Earth steady - sometimes it didn't.

Thomas Hardy wrote that the peninsula (Portland) was carved by time out of a single stone. Purbeck is only half a place of stone. Yet it would seem that both Isles had peeped on Medusa. Houses, roofs, porches, fuel houses, privies (not privy buckets), sinks, pigsties, garden walls, stiles, drinking troughs, grass rollers, even a quarry trundle wheel ... all of stone. A stranger might wonder if the extraction of so much stone might not have scarred the landscape. The answer is that it little more than bruised it, since quarrying *was* only moderately incursive.

In his book 'Highways and Byways in Dorset', Sir Fredrick Treves described the coastline after leaving Swanage as 'drab and savage'. He singled out Winspit Gap as a particularly 'lonely tragic spot', with just a castaway house and boat. This is a good representative area of *momento mori*. For tradesmen must have asked of other quarrymen worldwide, how long is this going to last, Purbeck stone and not another, stone and not brick, stone and not wood?

The decline of the quarries hereabout, and fall of many, has been described earlier in this discourse. The existing 'caves' were the old cliff quarries. Work in these ceased over forty

Eric Bower

years ago. Some were mere gashes into the white stone, whilst others 'go back' as far as one hundred and fifty feet. Of these longer ones, most are supported by huge pillars, their dark green and black colouring casting an eerie light around. Other cave roofs are held up by rickety-looking columns, imaginatively like the vertebrae of arthritic dinosaurs.

Another cave has its entrance outlined with yet another mineral, 'ink washed' in straight lines, architectural looking, resembling the entrance of a cubist cathedral. Purbeck would not be Purbeck if it did not have surprises.

There is a cave of irony, green screened by ivy, steel barred and surrounded by concrete. Local people knew this cave by the name of Port Arthur. Port Arthur - why? nobody knows. Of all the Port Arthurs around the world, only one seemed to fit. A Port Arthur from whom only tales escaped. The terrible 19 century penal colony in Tasmania. This seemed appropriate, as it would have been convicts' work to transport stone from this remote cave to a waiting barge. The owner of the cave was a man named Johnny Turner, whisky drinker, quarryman, and sub-postmaster, a stamp's lick away from the rest of the world.

Now, Winspit's Port Arthur is home to a colony of very rare Greater Horseshoe bats, largest bat in England. 'Protected', a notice says, 'by law'. That he was mindful of theft, (formerly punishable by transportation) was obvious, for all his tools were deeply branded with the initials J.T., even his pit props, J.T. Finally, for some 'castaways', Winspit Caves were better than the abandoned hope of a workhouse. Rather than exist in such a place, men, old men, simply rendered themselves back into the rock. Unknown, unprotected by any law (unlike the Greater Horseshoe bat). Today, we are anxious to pass laws to preserve little jungles, drab savage places, to be a little untidy again.

On the Isle of Portland there are many abandoned 'quarry gardens', great banks of stone, overgrown opencast areas, a paradise for wildlife. Why not the same on the Isle of Purbeck? Abandoned green wilderness not Trusts or Heritage. Maybe this is impossible in Purbeck because we have not the vast quantities of maiden rock. On Portland there are more tons of

Port Arthur - Winspit

stone 'lying around' than have ever been dug in Purbeck. Purbeck has had to be content with smaller havens of neglect along the old quarry roads, where butterflies bask on warm stones, fat woodpigeons 'clatter' frantically in drowning ivy, burgeoning wild fruit blossom like tiny scented lights, and far above, a buzzard quarters rock and lynchet.

Generally, our instinctive love of high ground is atavistic and spiritual. This is the very essence of why stone is quarried; beauty rather than ugliness being the aim of the mason ... and why we look up at the night sky. Stone is an edifier, it draws our gaze along a cathedral nave and our hands over the smoothness of a sculptured head - it s the encompassed vastness of eternity's matter. Atavism is 'life' in the air. It sees the wind, smells the snow, knows the elements are wearing away our place of standing. The 'mystery of life', as it comes towards us, shoots by and continues - where? Where ends the note of a fluting bird, the dying chord of an anthem, the hiss of expanding space? Some physicists think it possible for mind to be in two places at once. Perhaps time is the life everlasting.

The universe is elegant and fashionable ... what else ... Purbeck quarrymen ... Purbeck quarrymen?

The turning world turns people by degrees. For instance, the degree needed to change a working man's lifestyle. Let us consider the words - style, fashion - Purbeck quarrymen, who worked in narrow mud paint veins, wore moleskin trousers, thick white fustian, with straps below the knee, flannel shirt, hobnail boots, and a wide leather belt with a brass buckle - worn around his belly more than his waist for abdominal support, giving him an almost 'O.K. Corral' appearance. The nadir of fashion. For some men, especially the young, it must have seemed a moleskin existence, a yellow moleskin existence, and, maybe as an act of defiance, some men overdressed between home and their quarr hole. Nearly all wore a bowler hat and walked with a swagger.

But the real fashion spin-off was from the quarrymen who went to work in London as monumental masons. These masons were an élitest clique in the heart of London. At the wave of a tailor's needle a new phenomenon was created - the quarryman dandy. And, when a sparky dandy came back to his homeland, he probably wore a black bow-tie, striped trousers (like a guardsman), polished shoes, a fashion cut overcoat, leather gloves, and a white scarf. Even old men used to have their suits made to measure, of navy blue pilot cloth. This clean clothes 'uniform' differentiated city stone masons from the rough-styled Purbeck quarrymen who preferred to bide whom.[2]

In Thomas Hardy's 'Return of the Native', Clym Yeobright (the native), a product of the heath, goes away to work in the precious stone trade in Paris. He returns home a sorry man and says to a group of heth[3] simpletons, "I thought our life here as contemptible, to oil your boots instead of brushing them, to dust your coat with a switch instead of a brush". Clym is all for 'dressing down' for Egdon. He longs for the oil and the switch again.

Many masons became businessmen - with their own monumental stonemason's yard - others returned home. Some had married London girls, girls with cat vowels and quick ways - though they were not all 'cockerneys', as one man said. One wonders what those wives thought of their once smart men, who returned to close their days in a quarry (few men retired). Now, no longer just a brush-off of stone dust but a man in a huge fustian nappy and a Stan Laurel bowler hat.

1920s - beginning of the 'bird-bath' industry

My reader might ask - what has all this to do with the stone trade? It's 'near' history, and the problem with near history is that people can't relate to it, it's too near. The 'distant past' was well documented in so far as it was, but, just beyond human memory. There is a plethora of records but little of it relatable today. Most of this discourse is trying to shed some light on near history that is between (almost) forgotten memory and records.

Footnotes
1. viviparus: Purbeck marble is predominately bluish limestone, rarer, red and green, crowded with the freshwater pond snail, *viviparus*.
2. dialect for stay at home
3. heth: heath

Chapter 4

ROMANCE AND REALITY

The Romans were well dug in in Purbeck - though there is little trace of them above ground. So, in the dim light of recent history, let us do a 'dig' on ourselves. What was the ethos of a quarry area? A lot of sentimental guff has been written (especially by the Victorians) about an Englishman's home. There was no place like it. Most English working-class people lived in slums in the great cities, and hovels in the countryside. In the period after the First World War enormous hardship was experienced by all but the better off and downright wealthy. Only they thought depression and slump was father at the breakfast table with a hangover. But at last in the cities those sweet homes were pulled down and council houses built. That was probably the most important enactment of the first Labour Government of 1924.

Purbeck quarrymen had little hand in that great programme - though indirectly they had, through municipal contracts and public works. Most Purbeck stone went for private house building, church fabric, landscaping ... the middle class displaying their rewards in mortared stone. As I wrote earlier in this discourse - in the 18th and 19th centuries, a quarryman could build his own home for a few pounds. After the Great War, the desire to 'build your own' was not contemplated. It would have been more expensive, and maybe the war had exhausted men's efforts. Did the carnage and destruction of conflict leave men psychologically and physically enervated? In the shanty parish of Worth Matravers (for example), from the early 1920s to the early 1950s, there were a great number of 'temporary homes'. Hutments of galvanised iron were erected in a few days, and most unlikely of all, eleven railways carriages, bought for about £25 each, housed families living in the village of Worth Matravers.

Some folk had first-class carriages, some third. You can't get away from class distinction. They made excellent homes

Quarryman's Hut

because, although rather narrow, they were dry, and best of all in a windy village, draught proof. The most bizarre hovels were out of sight, a few quarry caves commandeered by recalcitrant old men, not a bad billet if you are not too fussy.

Now almost all those temporary dwellings have gone - though they have risen again as quarrymen's huts. In the fullness of time, most will be 'clad' with stone, making them home sweet home for fax machines and computers.

Perhaps we should ask ourselves what limit expediency? How deeply would the pockets of the wealthy be lined before the quarryman understood the depths of his own exploitation? How long before phrases such as 'the dignity of labour' assumed a hollow ring? 'To toil and not to seek for rest.' Many men and women in the Industrial Revolution lay down by their machines at night, to be ready to begin work at first light.

Imagine a place within the shores of Fair Albion, with no school, pub, church, chapel, shop, hall, village for the use of, reading room, post office -. A place unfriendly, sinister, roadless and lampless, cottages without the softness of thatch, built without square or plumb-line, functional and dark. Imagine, a footstep beyond the hamlet, huge mounds of thrown-up mud, like latter-day tumuli, huge scar banks, like the shells of countless giants' feasts ... and everywhere, descending, sliding, groping into the earth, an area exposed to sun, fog, and wind, heartless. And crawling around and down these mounds, children worked, women worked, and many men worked themselves to death - dead of sheer exhaustion. A place that knew no delicacy for women, no chance for children, no hope for men but the quarries. That place, and its time, was called Acton. West of this area was riddled with 'undergrounds' and some opencast quarries. I have always felt that writing meticulously about the Purbeck quarries and stone would be as boring to the reader as studying a railway timetable written on the back of an Ordnance Survey map. Well, God help me, this is Acton Common.

The beds of stone hereabouts are - from top to bottom - Rag, which, according to location, could be crumbly or very good. The next bed is Grub, which again varied from stone no better than hard core to reasonable stuff. Roach again varied according to where you quarried it. Then the large Thornback bed, a sort of blue hued stone - up to ten feet long. Lower still the Whetsun bed, the harder part of which was very good stone, and finally the Freestone, the undisputed best stone.

Some of the underground quarries, quite near the surface, ran but a matter of yards, others maybe around in a crescent, a few went straight ahead. One, I was told, ran for over half a mile. One tale told by a quarryman was that some of the undergrounds twixt Acton and Worth were so near the surface that they could hear sheep nibbling grass above their heads.

The ethos of Acton was no society - no camaraderie of many men going underground to work. The little undergrounds didn't live like a large mine being worked, and, perhaps most telling, the Acton quarries as elsewhere were family affairs - and family affairs can be pretty grim. Earlier I described what Acton hadn't; now in a few sentences I want to 'paint' Acton as it was about the turn of the century.

It was an odd place. Cottages built on all sorts of different levels, facing all directions, no layout or plan. Most families kept a few chickens, had a pile of lobster pots, had back yards - high and walled in. From outside, the hamlet, especially north to south, looked like a Crusader castle. Most cottages had their own well. Being a 'dark' hamlet, it was arcane. Everywhere there was a corner around which you could turn, some cottages had a smuggler's cache hole. An old person today remembered it as a poor place - not much was known about it. Land to the west of Acton was known locally as Acton Common. It was still mostly unenclosed. By day it was a typical common - smooth grass, gorse bushes, skylarks' nests, watchful ponies, adders and butterflies. By night, men were abroad with snares and nets, boots pounding the earth, a momentary flash of a lantern, the dull snick of a rabbit's neck broken, or a pheasant's alarm call - like a learner driver crashing an old gearbox ... and the wind howling and blowing in the blackness. Fustian and stubble, bar and candle, exhaustion and death - no wonder all paths led out to the next village pub ... it was their only solace. Their grim lives were preordained; though born to an area many hundreds of feet about sea level, they went - or were driven - straight to the bottom - like a man fallen into a tidal sea.

Blacklands (old Eng. Blaec) south-east of Acton

There was no life enlightenment for the quarrier, no hope of it, no need of it. There was work at Blaec Land, nothing more, even though his path to quarr was spangled with glow-worms. Early visitors to Purbeck usually skirted deep manmade holes, with only a silent grey donkey in sight, they had not the appeal of 'real caves'. Real caves are mysterious places, full of bats and a lingering aroma of strong spirits on the dank air. But a quarry - no, that was where men worked ... there was nothing romantic about that.

But what now - in this era of neo-realism? When Britain lost her colonies and was spoken of as a second-rate power, it was mooted in some quarters that we should turn the country into one huge glazed-over museum. The old industrial factories, cotton mills and coal mines open to the public. Let them see where the Victorian work ethic began. The idea found little support.

Suburban Simulation of Rural Reality

Our past is something we are not sure about. At one moment we swell our chests to the strains of 'Rule Britannia', at other, uneasy moments, doubt creeps in as we read about the appalling horrors of 18th and 19th Century industrial and pastoral life. Yet we take for granted what is under our feet. The cities and large towns had crossing sweepers - to allow the respectably shod to cross a road. Today, we have pavements, kerbs, channels and setts for everybody. Much of that stone supplied from the underground quarries of Purbeck. So, it often comes down to the question ... to expose boldly or to conceal. Gradually Purbeck is diminishing. Stone leaves it every day. Great holes in the landscape testify to that. Oil is pumped out by the rolling barrel, and blue china clay trundles off by road and rail. In some places their diminishment is noticeable. An old china clay miner told me that, when he was a young man, his bedroom window looked out on to the summit of Creech Barrow. It disappeared from view many a long year ago, he said.

Creech Barrow - 654ft above sea level

Man made banks of earth to screen quarries - as directed by Dorset County Council

Quarrymen work in a natural way. Stacking stone where it is easiest to load on to lorries or leaving to weather. No quarrier wants to make hard work harder. This leaves the National Trust, the largest landowner in Purbeck, in a quandary. The National Trust is a tidy body. It doesn't like too many piles of stone against the skyline, or old gates - 'a vallen to'. Gates, smelling new, must be five barred ... acorn signs lead you over well-made stiles, tombstones direct, miles from or to go, earth banks screen, advice to quarrymen on how to stack stone neatly is freely given ... in short, a civilised ethos for the rambler, or green welly, dog and stick brigade. Like a second coming, the policy of the National Trust is to make all things new.

This is good old predictable history repeating itself. A tourist guide dated 1902 and issued by the Swanage Advertising Committee, was entitled 'Healthy Pretty Swanage'. It went into paeans about the climate, the scenery, the number of private schools, sea bathing, boating, fishing and golf club ... where indeed better for a holiday or permanent residence? The Purbeck quarrymen are a feature, the guide says, they have still their old customs and restrictions. They are underground too, not unsightly. This 'spin-off', the local character, the men who told yarns taller than their pewter pots. The man who collected 'visitors' in a carriage and took them around the local beauty spots and told such stories that the carriage was often seen to rock, more with laughter than the bumpiness of the road. Perhaps this is how the image of bumpkinism gained ground - but if 'newcomers' cared to pay for listening to the art of storytelling, that was their business.

It is interesting to follow the tendrils of the mind, sometimes they cleave, sometimes they reach higher. A loose-end tendril was remembering the old brown coloured picture postcards. This 'wish you were here' trade began in the late 19th Century in most seaside towns. The postcard trade took longer to reach rural areas. It was after the First World War that the village shop at Worth Matravers sold postcards at one penny each. A photographer was commissioned to take local 'views'. He went everywhere, even, it was said, to the top of the lime kiln at Swanworth Quarries to get a good shot of Combe Bottom through to Chapman's Pool. Yet how many photographs do you imagine he took of the small quarries and quarriers compared to healthy pretty views ... ? As telling was a word association. The process used by the photographer was on bromide paper - used in printing from a negative. Bromide - a sedative ... and that was what the rural scene postcards were - 'sedatives', lulling, peaceful, pretty, far from life. Where has modern photography taken us now, where does the photographer swing his camera when he is at the top of a kiln, for the moral shot will always crackle, burn and bubble - even if out of sight. Yet the photographer (intrepid fellow) was not the only artist around. The Isle of Purbeck was not only rambled over by muscular Christians with thumb sticks and sandals, but by the second wave of 'theatricals', painters, poets, colour experiencers, seeking campy chat, cider, yokel worship, and cheap cottages to rent. How many of these lithe fellows painted, wrote, recorded, life in an underground, in a 19th Century quarrier's cottage, loading stone into a barge off a cliff face ... where has the artist set Purbeck?

This discourse calls for nothing except, maybe, a holding out for the old vernacular tongue - or vulgar tongue, as the historians called it. Some truths about old Purbeck need to be seen rather than read about. So with this in mind, may I suggest a walk from Kimmeridge to Anvil Point - carrying with you a vulgar old map?

After some decent coastline names; Swyre Head, Freshwater Steps, Egmont Point ... (probably because they were landowners' seaboards), you will come on to 'Robust Purbeck'. The names of the cliffs and rocks almost shout at you, as if Purbeck itself is holding up a piece of rock and defying the world with it, for you have left the neat and tidy tongue behind. Now, names are rough as sea kale. Green Pit and Shit Yallery Hole, Scratch Arse, Smoking Hole, Ring Bum Gardens ... Yet even more than robustness there is a sense, not only of belonging, but stake tide - to stake out against the incoming tide.

Let the great and the good have buildings and public works (of stone) named after them, but a greater eponymy is an area itself. Tilly Whim (cliff quarries), Mike and Whilly's Cave and watch rock, Mike's Corner and quarr, Blacker's Hole, Bowers Rock, and their chaplain, St Aldhelm, and perhaps the most synonymous of all, the topographer of the living map, William Jeremiah Bower ... or, to all who knew him - in Purbeck and beyond, as Billy Winspit - fisherman and quarryman.

The name Purbeck is obscure. The most probable derivation, Hutchins says, is from pure and beck - a rivulet from the number of little clear springs that issue off the foot of the hills all over the Island. There are other derivations - like a parson's sermon, thirdly, fourthly ... Many sources were secondary, because primary sources were often written (for one reason or another) with a forked quill. This is where the dialect tongue, though not without 'fault', was useful. It was the tongue used in the main industry of the Island, quarrying for marble and stone. Though dialect was the spoken word, a lexicographer would have found great difficulty in understanding the different meanings of words between village and village, even between families. But much 'meaning' has been lost through abuse, neglect, even shame. Thus when a writer (after dutiful research) writes about the Lannen Vein lane and end, or Laning Vein, of stone - does he mean the Leaning Vein? Was the Downs Vein so called because it was mainly quarried on Downland? Semantics are all round us - like scars[1]. Scars lead us on, as words will - to a world trying to heal its ills by being neat and tidy, precise and clean. In 'The Devils' Dostoyevsky writes of Holy Russia as a country of wood, most people living in tumbledown shacks. In Europe, theirs is a country of stone, he writes; 'They still have something to lean on there.'

The Future

Having wallowed in the past - where else can the history of an old industry begin? May I now wallow in the future of the stone industry? What of it? Today, the overall ethos of the quarry trade is hopeful. There seems to be a return to older, steadier ways - not 'little inches', but consensus building - where architects, local authorities, the National Trust, people at ground roots level, play their part.

There will always be a market for Purbeck stone, especially

Crusher - Swanworth Quarries 1920's

around London. Encouraging too are the number of municipal authorities who are moving away from granite kerbs and tarmac, back to stone. 'Purbeck' is not short of competitors. Bath and Portland, with their firms of solemn looking young masons, rather overshadow little Purbeck, and many of the Yorkshire quarries, where the stone is like our own, rival with more than northern grit.

Locally, there will always be landscape gardens, garden centres, house building ... the stone affairs I wrote about at the beginning of this discourse. Today in 1994 there is a steady demand ... 'enough work on'. There is less frenzy - the aggressive, greedy 1980s scramble for Purbeck seems over. But not before it has left its mark.

Recently, I visited a place gouged out of the landscape.[2] A vast, moon white crater, with a few 'toy' plant around - bright green against the white dust. Nothing moved. At the crater's rim, a few fat rabbits ran, and magpies, like feathers stuck into cotton reels, slanted around. Here an old tyre, there a 1930s black mudguard. Huge vertebrae tracks of some lumbering vehicle lay, double toed, across the quarry floor. But most derelict of all was an old crusher, left almost as a memento -

dilapidated and rusted. Suddenly a faint breeze stirred - loose sheets of galvanised iron tipped against each other ... tip, tip tip, ... tip. Where ever you hear that sound, it is the unmistakable sound of abandoned industry. Tip, tip tip, ...

Footnotes:
1. scars: small chips of waste stone
2. The enormous area of depredation north west of Worth Matravers began as a quarry no larger than a church porch. Its owner, John Brown sold it to a company called Worth Quarries in 1920. The company was Bournemouth based. Worth Quarries installed plant for crushed stone, tar macadam, and hard-core for roads. About 50 men were employed. The company went into liquidation in 1928. A former director with backers formed a company called Swanworth Quarries Ltd, a combination of the words Swanage and Worth. This company prospered until taken over by Tarmac Ltd in 1980.

ON THE ARTICLES

Transition always seems sudden, seeming so because this is the nature of change. Change thrust upon society was how life was in the 17th Century. The 'Good Old Cause' had gone down the public drain, and the gear wheels of industrial fury were soon to be cranked into action. Where were the quarrymen? They were at the supply end of demand and had to ask themselves two, if not more, important questions. One: what stone was leaving where, how, and to whom? Two: who were going to be their middlemen (merchants)? Quarrymen had gone to bed as Purbeck Marblers and woken up in the Market Place. It was not enough for members of a Craft Guild to gather around the Craft Box with bared heads, whilst the rules of the society were read out.

Large quantities of stone were demanded. Poor folk as well as rich folk begged brick and stone for town and city. Thus it was probable that the 'quarry hands' might have been divided as to how best to supply large quantities of good stone ... always the Industry's problem. Should they stay with the old ways at Corfe Ruin ... "and the many great evils that do daily attend future improvement and better management", or move eastward to Sandwich (Swanage)? 'Eastward look' won the day, though it would seem there was a pause for a while (slump) for stocks of stone to build up at Swanage.

Sandwich, especially with the opening roads, was obviously the better centre. Surely too it was sensible that stone should be shipped from where the bulk of it was quarried. As well it was a natural bay for shallow draught boats without much tidal movement, and directly facing the open sea.

Now should follow the crackle of roles of parchment with a flurry of historic dates, to give the trade respectability. But for all the pedants demand to know the exact hour of the drying of the ink, the earliest Articles recorded are March 1651/2[1], with Shrove Tuesday, the most important date in the marblers' calendar, hopping about like a bird on one leg.

1651/2, time of the Commonwealth and free state, a time to

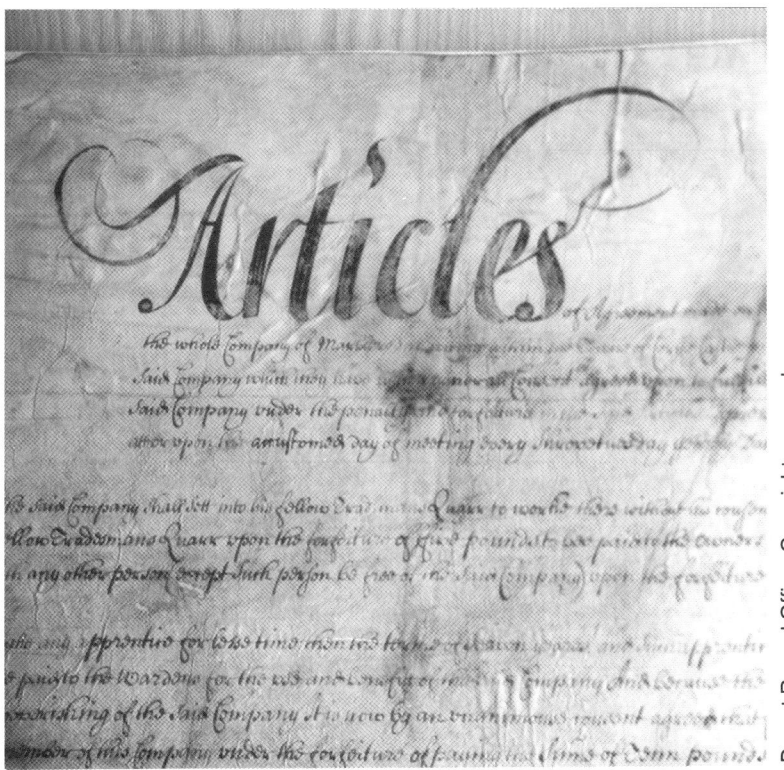

Articles of Agreement of the Purbeck Marblers and Stone Cutters - 1697/8

take a forward view rather than a backward glance, a time to infer. Customs and rights were probably thought to be in as much danger as the privileges and property of those on the wrong political side. The stone trade slumped after the Civil War, but not terminally.

The actual mechanics of getting the trade to 'move with the times' must have been difficult. The first record of this was in a set of Articles dated 1697/8[2], these Articles include a provision to set up a joint stock company based at Sandwich. Each quarryman to pool his stone. Yet it is significant that in 1695 quarrymen were hell bent on keeping the right of way to Ower Quay open. Maybe this was an insurance, in case Sandwich didn't 'come off'.

In 1695 a tribute of pepper (and a football) was paid to John

Collins of Ower confirming an agreement between the said John Collins and the Company of Free Marblers. The course of the way being as follows. Beginning at the said house of John Collins, at the east side, down along the lane (Peppercorn Lane) to the strand and so to the quay. Witnessed by Joseph Hort, Tho: Chapman Junior, and William Cull.

These names occur again in the 1697/8 Articles, in pursuance thereof have unanimously chosen - Thomas Chapman, Joseph Hort the Elder, Henry Serrell ... , to be the managers of the said joint stock trade. Men of 'known integrity and honesty' and not without a pound in their pockets. This was the spawning of the merchant class. The gradual move to Sandwich quickened the blood of commercialism, but did not 'free' the trade. Events veer, but seldom change the course of history. The merchant got richer and the quarryman was for ever beholden to him. No doubt this was due in part to their (the quarrymen's) attitude to work. A 'free' man who swaggered to work in a bowler hat, laughed at Sisyphean tasks, and played games (of strength) with the stones after work, was not the type to fulfil an order dead on the stroke of when ever.

May I intrude for a moment on this discourse with my own surname. There are at least two Pushman's marks ⊓ on the 1651/2 parchment rolls. We, with many others had a hand in it. I found viewing the ten Articles, so carefully written, an experience out of time. The parchment, yellowing and thick, with faded writing the colour of colour of cold tea.

The Mason's marks, like twisted rusty nails - the mark was the man. So much endeavour and intent written just before Cromwell became Lord Protector. History is like splintered glass, you have to turn it this way and that before you can see through its tell-tale refractions. The Articles themselves are very 'run of the mill'. Their regulations were of the minutest character. No 'outsiders', disobedience of their orders was punished by fines, or in the last resort, expulsion, which involved the loss of right to trade ... acceptance of any apprentice into the company... . One suspects other old Craft Guilds have such articles and go through similar ritual performances on certain days. For instance Lead Mining in the Peak District. There were certain specific laws which had to be observed.

These laws were enforced stringently, and many of them seem unfair. One now required that the mine be continually worked but this was sometimes impossible due to bad health or other commitments. However failure to comply could mean that a miner might lose his mine altogether.

A poem of the period, 1663, states that the penalty for being caught stealing the load ore for the third time was either a slow death by starvation or the loss of a hand. In Purbeck, quarrymen content themselves with fines or expulsion.

The 'Marblers'' article I find most interesting is no. 7, the last married man to bring a football 'according to the custome of our company', as was the provision of a pound of pepper. Presenting a pound of pepper and a football on Ash Wednesday to the tenant of Ower Farm preserved the ancient right of way. But why? A common token was a red rose, two fat hens, but pepper? Even Frederick Treves in his 'Highways and Byways of Dorset' wrote 'A pound of pepper and a football form a curious commercial instrument, of which the chronicler furnishes no explanation'. Maybe it was not unusual to the King's castle, the pepper at any rate[3].

Which still leaves the bouncing football. Football is a very old game, played as early as the 14th Century[4]. Maybe this traditional 'diversion' had more to do with an even earlier, uglier, custom than just booting a ball[5]. All kinds of odd things get tacked on to 'rights' in the name of tradition.

From the 18th Century onwards many Associations were formed, but went to the wall. The last known was between the World Wars.

This Co-operative (Co-op) was made up of some dozen or more quarrymen who ran a Co-op at Acton. It was quite well appointed. A huge galvanised iron shed, stone sheds, loading bankers, a shop (Tuck), and office with a telephone. Whilst it got away to quite a good start, by the early 1930s it was 'done for'. Yet another collapsed enterprise.

Thus brambles and time fold over old memories, like inlier rocks.

Footnotes:
1. The year began on 25 March until 1752 when it changed to 1st January - Lord

Chesterfield's Act
2. Copies of the Articles are common right up to the present day. Like the Shrove Tuesday football, there is always the last married man to bring one.
3. One William Scovill paid the King one pound of pepper per annum, with 12 pennies for enclosing a certain place of meadow. "Croft which Robert Scovill holds of our Lord the King by service of one pound of pepper per Annum".
4. (when a reign nearly stopped play). Football has long been associated with great violence, King James I tried to ban it - "Debarre from the court all rough and violent exercise as the football". At the city of Chester the Shrove Tuesday 'exercise' became so violent that it was replaced by a foot-race.
5. Who among older readers has not had a pint of mild and bitter at a Turk's Head pub? Turk is the sprung word. Swanage masons were once known as Turks to 'outside' masons. Even the old Swanage Football Club was called the Turks, a time to infer?

Articles 1651/2

Ffirst That no man of the Company shall set into his fellow-tradesman's Quarr to worke there without his consent within twelve moneths and a day nor to come into any part of that ground within a hundred foote of his fellow tradesman's Quarr upon the forfeiture of ffive poundes to be paid unto the owner of the quarr unto whom the offence shall be dun. Neither shall no man in this company worke partners with any man, except it be a freeman of the same company, upon the forfeiture of ffive poundes.

Seconly That no man in the company shall take any Apprentice but that he shall keep him in hiw owne house uprising and downe lying for the terme of Seaven years upon the forfeiture of ffive poundes to be paid unto the Wardings of the company for the use and benefitt of the whole Company.

Thirdly That no man after his Apprentice shall take any other Apprentice in the shole terme of seaven years upon the forfeiture of ffive poundes for every moneth for as many moneths as he shall keepe him: and to be paid to the Wardings for the use of the Company.

Ffowerthly That no man in this company shall sell or make sale of any Stone within this Island but by his owne proper name, upon the forfeiture of ffive poundes To be paid unto the Wardings for the use of the company That no man of our Company shall under-creep his fellow tradesman to take from him any bargaine of work of his trade upon the forfeiture of ffive poundes. To be paid to the Wardings of the Company for the use and benefitt of the whole Company.

ffivethly That every man in our Company upon notice from the Wardings of the Company by the Stewards To appeare at any place appoynted and doe not there appear according to order shall paie for his neglect Three shillings ffower pence To be paid unto the Wardings for the use and benefit of the Company, without a very Lawful excuse. And that noe man of our Companie shall take any Apprentice that shall be base born or of parents that are of loose lyfe upon the forfeiture of ffive poundes To be paid to the Wardings of the Companie for the use and benefit of the whole Company: or that the said servant or apprentice is or have been a Loose liver.

Sixthly That upon any aceptance of any apprentice into the Company He shall paie unto the Wardings for the use of the Company Six shillings eight pence a penny loafe and two pots of beere. That no man of the said Company shall set a Laborer worke upon the forfeiture of ffive poundes.

Seaventhly That any man in our Company the Shrovtewsdaie after his marriage shall paie unto the Wardings for the use and benefit of the Company twelve pence and the last married man to bring a foot-ball according to the Custome of our Company.

Eightly That upon any appointed meeting at any time or at any place together ther shall any noyse, hindrance, or disturbance to the Company, upon the command silence from the Wardings and not observed, the man in default shall paie twelve pence to the wardings for the use & benefit of the Company.

Ninthly, That the Wardings of the country shall have the Company's Stocke: always provided that the Warding of the towne shall have securytie for ye use and benefit of the Company.

Tenthly, That if any of our Company shall at any time reveale or make knowne the secrets of this Company or any part thereof, upon notice given and just proofe be made, he shall pay for his default to the Wardings for the use and benefit of the Companie five poundes.

We, whose Names are hereunder written being a Company of Marblers or Stone Cutters doe by theis presents binde ourselves and every and either of us respectively joyntly and severly, and the heires executors and assignes of us and every and eyther of us respectively joyntly and severly in the sum of Tenn Poundes of Lawful English money, To allow and maintaine All the said Articles above mentioned And upon the breach of any one of these

Articles we doe all consent and allow uphold and maintaine that the Offender or Breach-maker of any of theis Articles shall pay according unto the ffyne of the article for his offence, or shall be putt by his trade, and no man in our Company to deale with him, untill he shall give satisfaction for his faulte doun unto his Company of Marblers or Stone Cutters. And we doe likewise binde ourselves, our heires, executors, and assignes for ever, That ye Offender shall paie according to the breach of the article agreed on for his offence, or be put by his trade, and no man in the Company to deale with him untill he shall give satisfaction for his fault soe doun unto his Company of Marblers or Stone Cutters To these and every and eyther of these Articles Clauses and agreements before mentioned and expressed we doe binde our selves our heires executors and assignes and every and eyther of us respectively in the forfeiture of Tenn Poundes of good and Lawful English money for the use and benefit of the Company of Marblers or Stone Cutters To allow uphold and maintaine all these Articles agreed on

In witnesse whereof we have hereunto putt our hands and scales, the day and yeare above written.

[Here follow names. And about a hundred years later, the signature is added of

Antho: ffurzman,
Maior, a° 1655]

ADDENDUM

A Ruse By Any Other Name

This discourse, Purbeck Underground, has had a 'key' word running through it, as from a stone to a stone. The word is Charter.

The Charter was said to have held that Purbeck quarrymen had a right to be independent and dig for stone wherever they would on the Island.

What is the evidence of this? There is no empty charter chest, or particular place where it was known to have been kept, there is only time.

The building of Corfe's castle was an 'ongoing' business. It was begun at a time, 'so ancient as without a date', and continued to be built, pulled down and rebuilt, almost up to the time of its destruction.[1] Henry III was a master builder of much of the castle as well as an extractor of a vast quantity of King's marble for Westminster Abbey.

Here then we are beginning to collect evidence enough to see how the idea of a Royal Charter could have come about ... by long association. Such a charter, if granted then would have been deep-rooted in mediaevalism. If later in time, it would have been a useful document, almost a rite of passage.

Since 'castle time' Corfe must have been a good place to live. It was an ancient Borough, and the inhabitants enjoyed 'many amenities and privileges'. Also the 'Castle' paid well above the going rate in wages. Rough masons and craftsmen must have candle clocked in with alacrity.

I suspect serious 'talk of a charter', an enabling charter, began after the shift of the stone industry away from Corfe to the area of Worth, Acton Common, Langton and Swanage. The 'political' status quo had changed. The quarrymen would have been more out on an Island limb, as well as losing the patronage of the Castle. The paradox is that only when the industry went underground to quarry was it thought expedient to bring a Charter to light. The 1651/2 Articles don't even hint of one.

For centuries this document has hovered in quarrymen's minds. Many claim familiarity with it, explain its absence variously as lost, stolen, loaned, sold, burnt. It is a fact that early records of the marblers seemed to have been burnt at Corfe Castle in a fire about 1680. Also many books and papers, 'at ye value of 1,300£s' were pillaged from the Castle after the slighting. So, to be fair to history, there *could* have been a Charter. But more probably the marblers and stone cutters owed much to the old custom of the manor, custom of the Castle, (custom was always a good thing to have on your side) ... and latterly the understanding between Bankes and the quarrymen. Bankes the proprietor knew that the men who dealt in 'little inches and stone pennies' were unlikely to wrest more from the earth than a meagre living. All they asked was 'the right of living by labour'.

Man is not everywhere in chains - but everywhere linked. (Coincidentally?) "Corfe is an ancient borough. Its Mayor is, by virtue of his office, a magistrate, and the members of its Corporation, as long as it had one, were called barons"[2]. This is interesting because, when the Barons of England drew up the Great Charter, the ensuing rights they claimed for themselves they claimed for the nation. The forfeiture of the freeman on conviction of felony was never to include his tenement, or that of the merchant his wares, or that of the countryman his wain, (the quarryman his quarry). The 'spirit of Magna Carta'.[3]

Actual evidence of 'custom', and ambiguity from the Castle itself: In the reign of Edward I, from the 'Plea Rolls', one William Clavel brought an action against Elyas de Rabayne, the Constable of the Castle, in that he caused a quarry to be dug on the property of the said William at Holne, and there carried away stone for the works of the Castle. Elyas acknowledged the taking and justified on the plea that the Constable had a right of custom to cut timber and dig stone throughout the warren for repairs to the Castle. The jury said it was lawful for every Constable of the said Castle to take timber thereof when necessary, this being the custom of the Castle. Damages to the amount of one mark[4] are given for the oaks and for the stone taken.

M. Bizley

Finally it was the ethos of the hour. There were 'stretches of authority'. Constables of the Castle claimed many rights by custom, Parliamentary leaders appropriated for their private use...

Surely then quarrymen hewing down into God's earth must have seen it as right enough.

Footnotes:
1. We should remember that building work was very protracted, especially a castle. Workmen took their time. The 'dinner hour' stretched into the summer siesta, night work was never allowed (too dangerous and difficult to supervise) and labour was often pressed. Sometimes work ceased altogether. An example of this protraction was the nave of Westminster Abbey which was 150 years in the building. King Alfred had a single tower castle at Corfe in 875.
2. Picturesque Rambles in the Isle of Purbeck by C E Robinson MA, Barrister at Law.
3. The Great Charter, spawned by previous Charters, followed by additions.
4. Approx. six shillings and eight pence.

Bibliography

Author	Title	Place and Date of Publication
Stuart Morris	Portland	Wimborne, 1985
Hobbes Thomas	Leviathan	1651
W.M. Hardy	Old Swanage and Purbeck	Dorset County Council, 1910
Emmeline Hardy	The Story of Corfe Castle	Wimborne, 1988
R.J. Saville	The Stone Quarries of Langton Matravers	Langton Matravers History and Preservation Society Booklet No. 15, 1976
R.J. Saville	Ancient Order of Purbeck	Booklet No. 10, 1973
G.M. Trevelyan	British History in the 19th Century and after: 1782-1919	Longmans, Green & Co Ltd; 1922 + 1937
Eric Benfield	Purbeck Shop	Cambridge University Press, 1940
Hutchins	History of Dorset (Vols 1-3)	1868
Frederick Treves	Highways and Byways in Dorset	1906
Stewart Borrett	Swanage Rediscovered	Swanage, 1979
W.J. Arkell MA, DSC (with contributions by C.W. Wright MA & H J Osborne	The Geology of the County around Weymouth, Swanage and Lulworth	London HMSO, 1947
J.R. Green	A Short History of the English People	London, 1926
The Purbeck Soc. Papers	Read to that Society in the Years - 1855 and 1859	
D. Knoop and G P Jones	The Mediaeval Mason	Manchester University Press
C.E. Robinson	Picturesque Rambles in the Isle of Purbeck	London, c. 1882
T. Hardy	The Return of the Native	Macmillan 1st Ed., 1878
H.P. Smith	Memories of Ower	The Dorset Year Book

Tape Recording:
Jimmy Chinchen and Ralph Bower talking to John Dean about quarrying and Swanage life - 1977